IMAGES OF WALES

RHYL

Rhyl's coat of arms offers an enlightening impression of the town's history. The shield shows a ship and salmon, implying the boating and fishing traditions of the district. At the top of the crest is a Welsh lion, holding the arms of Rhyl. It is standing on a 'hill' or 'hillock' and implies the origins of the word Rhyl. The tawny colour known as 'tenny' is visible in a colour version of the arms. This colour is indicative of the sandy beaches and it is rarely ever used in armorial bearings, indeed these are the only arms in the British Isles to use tenny. The Welsh motto *'Yr Hafan Deg Ar Fin Y Don'* translates into English as 'the fair haven at the edge of the waves'. Rhyl Urban District Council was granted these armorial bearings in 1967 and they were inherited in 1974 by Rhyl Town Council, its successor authority.

IMAGES OF WALES

RHYL

DAVE THOMPSON

First published in 2006 by Tempus Publishing Limited

Reprinted in 2011 by
The History Press
The Mill, Brimscombe Port,
Stroud, Gloucestershire, GL5 2QG
www.thehistorypress.co.uk

British Library Cataloguing in Publication Data.
A catalogue record for this book is available from the British Library.

ISBN 978 0 7524 3783 5

Typesetting and origination by Tempus Publishing Limited.
Printed and bound in Great Britain by
Marston Book Services Limited, Didcot

Contents

Acknowledgements

I would like to record my appreciation to the many individuals and organisations who generously provided photographs, shared memories or freely parted with factual material for use in this book. I am indebted to Audrey Ballyn Davies, Elva Ballyn Stables, Pauline Ballyn Jones, Christ Church United Reformed church, Susan Clayton, John Glover, Val Hughes, Alun Jones, John Glyn Jones, Museum of the Royal Pharmaceutical Society, Graham Owen, Andrew Pierce, St Thomas' church, Jess Yates' estate, Dave Ramsbottom, Rhyl Golf Club, Rhyl Hockey Club, Rhyl Silver Band, Rhyl Town Council, Simmons Aerofilms, Ysgol Dewi Sant and the staff of Rhyl Library, Museum and Arts Centre for their goodwill and support. I have studied the history of many towns and found the people of Rhyl to be the warmest and most inviting folk I have yet encountered, not only in their openness but in the willingness they had to share old photographs and memories.

Once again I am indebted to George Teare for his work in checking my manuscript and to Serena Daroubakhsh for her tireless effort in tracing images and other likely sources. I followed every lead she offered and was invariably rewarded for my efforts.

To the memory of Christine Newby, 1957-1980

Introduction: Sunny Rhyl

A cursory glimpse at a map of old Denbighshire will reveal Rhyl did not exist until after the turn of the nineteenth century. The area was nothing more than a shallow isthmus of marshland scrub situated between the eastern mouth of the River Clwyd and the sea.

Rhyl was born through a parliamentary Act in 1794 granting permission for prominent local landowners to drain and reclaim the marshes under the guise of the Marsh Embankment Trust. The development of Rhyl may well have taken a slower course but for the expanding fashions of people in the smoke-ridden industrial heartlands of England who were increasingly 'taking the air' at summer resorts. By 1807 twenty acres of coastline were being advertised for the then new-fangled craze of 'sea bathing'.

It was only a matter of time before the fledgling settlement would spring into life, and the impetus came in 1846 when a public meeting invited subscriptions to develop the sea frontage with a terraced promenade. The work was completed with haste and within the year splendid villas were being built to form the East and West Parades. Rhyl's prosperity was sealed with the opening of the railway in 1848, allowing an ever increasing number of visitors to reach Rhyl. One guidebook of the day wrote of this fashionable water place, 'The salubrity of the air, the beauty of the scenery, the contiguity of the town to the sea, and the extent and firmness of the sands, render it a place of considerable attraction.'

The mid to late nineteenth century was a formative era and many new developments took place to satisfy the needs of visitors to the resort town. Victoria Pier opened in 1867 and the town's shopping streets were taking shape. By the turn of the century there were 1,833 houses and shops in Rhyl and this new fangled idea of using electricity to light streets was finding favour with the new Rhyl Urban District Council. With its fashionable promenade, top entertainment and a burgeoning number of hotels and boarding houses, Rhyl offered all the ingredients necessary to prosper as a resort. Allegedly even the weather favoured it! The milder temperate climate of the district was statistically tested and resulted in the much-marketed phrase 'Sunny Rhyl'.

Like many other towns Rhyl had earned fame for the endeavours and exploits of its inhabitants and visitors. In 1898 the pioneering film producer Arthur Cheetham brought images to life when he recorded a film of children playing on Rhyl sands. This was only three years after the Lumiere Brothers had given the world's first public film showing in Paris. In 1912 local aviator Vivian Hewitt won the pride and respect of the people of Rhyl when he became the first person to fly a plane across the Irish Sea. His arrival back home at Rhyl brought thousands of well wishers out onto the streets of Rhyl. One personality who drew little attention was T.S. Lowry. The famous painter of 'matchstick men and matchstick cats and dogs' knew Rhyl from fond boyhood memories of holidays here and returned in the 1920s to quietly paint scenes of the town.

The town grew considerably throughout the early part of the twentieth century. New settlers arrived and brought a close-knit spirit, evident in the plethora of churches, sporting and social societies that were flourishing. Indeed there are many clubs at Rhyl today that can still trace their origins back more than a century. By 1931 the population had soared to 13,000 – a fifty per cent increase on the inhabitants here twenty years earlier. Rhyl emerged unscathed from the Second World War and it served well its role as an evacuation centre for refugees and government departments, escaping the ravages of bomb blitzed cities.

The 1950s and 1960s heralded the era of the day tripper, made possible because the motor car became the mainstay of family travel. The Rhyl coast was a strong rival to Blackpool and other towns on the Lancashire coast but then some of its best-known features began to vanish. Rhyl Pier closed in 1966 and a few years later the magnificent Pier Pavilion was demolished. Tourism might have sustained Rhyl for over two centuries but even this has had its peaks and troughs; today the town has taken refuge in serving the affordable end of the holiday market. Few resorts have been able to compete against the public desire for overseas holidays.

Captured throughout this book are cherished resort scenes, landmarks, old modes of transport and glimpses of some of the key events and happenings from Rhyl's past. Some pictures were chosen to reveal how the town looked to past generations, others simply to stir the mind's eye. I hope you enjoy this impression of Sunny Rhyl.

Dave Thompson
August 2006

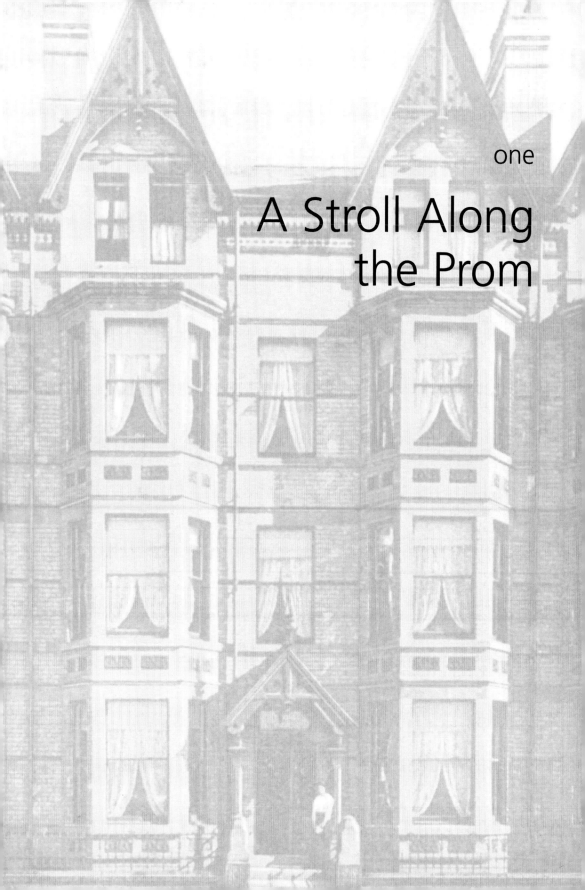

one

A Stroll Along
the Prom

Rhyl over 70 years ago.

An engraving of Rhyl from about 1840. The single-storey building to the far left is the Baths Hotel that had been built in the 1820s to accommodate the first visitors to the fledgling resort. This sketch provides an impression of how a young Rhyl looked before the construction of the promenade.

Another early engraving, this time from the 1880s. Lofty boarding houses now sprawl along the seafront of the shore and the artist has offered a rather fanciful impression of a steam ship sailing full speed into the pier. Steam packets brought sea passengers and cargo from as early as the 1820s, with daily services being offered to Rhyl from Liverpool's Pier Head and Mostyn.

Before the promenade was built the seafront was best known for its sand hills. Some areas of sand dune were still evident along the East Parade and Marine Drive in this postcard from 1909.

Promenade strollers pictured *c.*1907. The fountain to the left was a well-known feature of the prom, installed in 1862 to commemorate the coming of age of Conway Rowley of Bodrhyddan. It was removed in 1948 to make way for the Clock Tower.

A view along the stylish promenade in 1903. The opulent Queen's Palace underlined the prestige and glamour of Rhyl's seafront but sadly this marvellous pleasure palace was destroyed by fire in 1907.

Marine Drive in around 1909. The area beyond Marine Drive in the direction of Prestatyn had been known as 'splash point', and was at risk of major floods until 1951 when an extension of the sea wall was constructed.

WEST PARADE FROM ABBEY GARDENS, RHYL.

Above: The West Parade from Abbey Gardens. With a mile of lofty buildings, promenade, gardens and entertainment, Rhyl's seafront was considered one of the most resplendent resorts in Britain.

Right: Boarding establishments abounded in Victorian and Edwardian Rhyl. The East and West Parades and other roads off the promenade were bordered with lodging houses like Ferndale on the West Parade, pictured here in 1908.

"Ferndale" 75, West Parade, Rhyl. (Mrs. Fielding).

West Parade, Rhyl

Above: The scene along a traffic-free West Parade, *c.* 1910.

Left: A picture of Oakleigh on the Marine Drive. In Rhyl's 1947 guidebook its proprietor placed a full-page advert boasting that her premises provided hot and cold water in all bedrooms, something not then common to all establishments. There were about 200 boarding houses and hotels to be found in Rhyl at about this time.

The East Parade in 1913. The building to the right is the Westminster Hotel.

Today there is a large BMX and skateboard park situated on the promenade. It is a far cry from this 1926 picture showing children gently riding around on three-wheeled bicycles.

The children's paddling pool was quite a draw for youngsters but not seemingly on this cold day in the 1950s. Many promenade strollers have taken to the shelter and there is no activity around the pool. The end of Abbey Street can be seen on the top left corner of this picture.

The Promenade Gardens opened in 1908 and were an immediate success, with huge crowds of people visiting the site throughout the summer season.

Gardens and Bandstand from Pavilion. Rhyl

A good crowd of spectators watch Crown Green Bowls at the Marine Gardens, 1920.

In the Marine Gardens, Rhyl.

During the summer season daily concert performances were given at the bandstand. Sadly the sound of music in the sea air is something now missing from the traditional British seaside holiday.

Pictured here in 1936, the Pier Pavilion was the iconic symbol of Rhyl's stylish promenade. The 120ft high landmark could be seen as far away as Llandudno.

Kiosks were located along the promenade, serving up information, souvenirs and refreshments. Forrest's Ice Cream was one of the best-known kiosks, as was the Wire King – a trader who handcrafted ladies brooches from strands of wire. This prom view is from 1926.

Public competitions were used as another means of drawing the attention of holidaymakers, and there was a lot of fun to be had. Obstacle races generated a great deal of spectator interest as is evident in this picture from 1929.

WAR MEMORIAL, RHYL.

Rhyl's war memorial was erected in 1904 to commemorate those who had fallen in the Boer War. Since that time it has been resited in more than one location and new plaques have been added to mark the loss of local people in two World Wars. The memorial is pictured here at the East Parade, *c.* 1930.

The war memorial is pictured near to the Pier Pavilion in 1929.

Rhyl Silver Band performs alongside the war memorial on Remembrance Day, 1927.

A more modern scene at the war memorial. The Rhyl Silver Band are still offering musical accompaniment to the remembrance service in November 2005.

For many decades Punch and Judy shows were performed on the promenade. This postcard from 1910 shows a predominantly adult audience gathered to watch Professor Green's portrayal of the famous comic tragedy.

46613. RHYL: PUNCH ON THE PROMENADE.

That's the way to do it. Punch and Judy takes centre stage in this image from 1910.

CLOCK TOWER, RHYL

The promenade's Clock Tower was built in 1948 on the site previously occupied by the Conway Fountain. One feature that certainly never budged was the traditional Punch and Judy shows, pictured here still attracting a crowd in 1952.

This picture from 1913 shows the Gorsedd Circle near to the Royal Alexandra Hospital. The stones came from various parts of Clwyd and were installed for the National Eisteddfod in 1904. The stones were removed in the 1940s but re-erected for the return of the Eisteddfod in 1985.

The Marine Hydro opened in 1889 and was one of the most luxurious hotels on Rhyl's seafront.

Grange Private Hotel
EAST PARADE, RHYL

The Grange Hotel, *c.* 1955. It is one of the most prominent buildings on the East Parade and was originally known as Moranedd. So many of Rhyl's hotels have disappeared, yet the Grange Hotel is still open today and as popular as ever.

In 1980 Rhyl Sun Centre became the latest attraction to appear alongside the promenade. The £4.5 million centre is an exotic complex of indoor swimming pools and it was added to help bolster Rhyl's appeal to holidaymakers. This picture shows the interior of the complex in 1988.

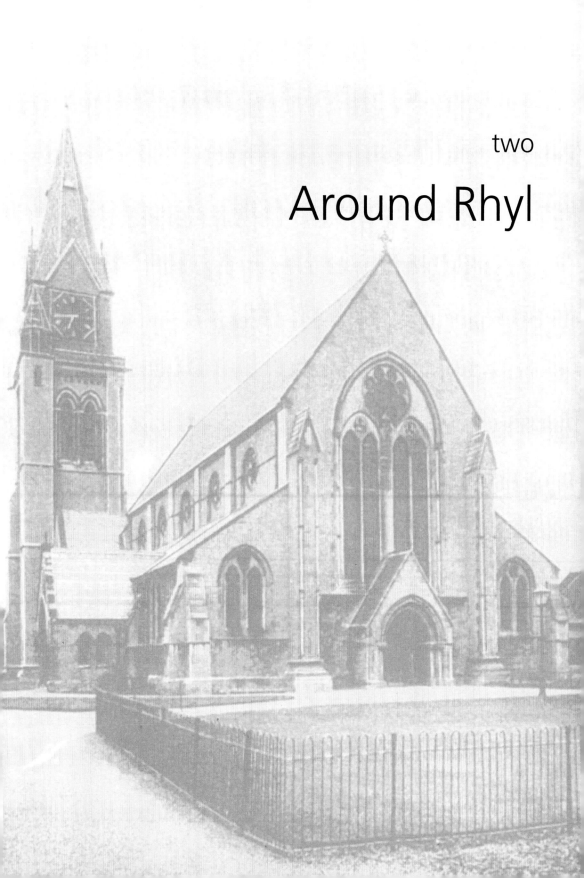

two

Around Rhyl

Brisk gossipy shops and a superb mix of goods were the hallmark of Rhyl's High Street, and it has
continued to be the focus of the town's retail hub for more than a century. This street scene dates from
around 1912 and shows High Street at the junction with Sussex Street.

High Street, 1908. Wide pavement verandas were an attractive feature of the Edwardian street scene. This
particular veranda concealed the Russell Buildings. Erected in 1891, these buildings accommodated many
well-known traders of the day, including Henkel's Toy Shop – one of the leading suppliers of Welsh dolls.

Above: A closer look down the street, *c.* 1922. The domed building to the right was occupied by the Constitutional Club, Star Supply Stores and the office of the photographer Wills Jones.

Right: A very rare view of Robert E. Price's dispensing chemist's shop in the High Street, 1900. The business was established in 1834 and sold a variety of powders and potions to cure all manner of ailments.

Looking down High Street from Vale Road Bridge, *c.* 1910. To the left was the Town Hall Stores and White Lion Hotel.

An early impression of Tom Lewis's White Lion Hotel, *c.* 1900. The hotel was demolished in the 1930s to make space for the Crosville Bus Depot in the High Street. Note the rather fine stone carving of a white lion above the main entrance to the hotel.

Horse–drawn carriages are seen outside North Wales Motors, 1908. The large hoarding advertises the Universal Bazaar: perhaps this is where bargain hunters went in those days?

Women pictured pushing prams along High Street, c.. 1931.

Wellington Road, Rhyl

Opposite above: In the very early days of Rhyl's transformation into a town Wellington Road was known as Quay Street. Viewed here in 1906 from the corner of High Street, it has continued to be one of the most commercially prosperous streets of the town. The corner shop on the immediate right of this picture is Hughes the tailors. Established in 1863, they were the oldest family firm in the district at the time this picture was taken.

Opposite below: Wellington Hall, 1893.

Right: Town Hall and Free Library in Wellington Road, *c.* 1910. The Town Hall building first opened in 1876 and an extension in 1907 added a library, part funded by the wealthy benefactor Andrew Carnegie. The magnificent granite building is now used for other purposes and Rhyl's Town Council is located at Wellington Community Centre.

Below: Queen Street, *c.* 1908.

Queen Street, Rhyl

An aerial view of the streets around Rhyl in 1971. St Thomas's church is a very noticeable feature in this picture.

33

Rhyl Bath Street & St Thomas Church

St Thomas Church, Rhyl.

Above: You can almost feel the humdrum nature of everyday life in this pre-First World War picture of Bath Street. Ladies are seen gossiping about the tittle-tattle of the day. The 203ft high tower and spire of St Thomas's church dominates the picturesque street scene.

Left: Undoubtedly the finest church in the district, St Thomas's parish church is one of the most commanding features of Rhyl. The construction of the church was estimated at £8,000 when work began in 1861. Construction progressed slowly, in fact so slowly that it was not completed until 1878, by which time it had cost more than three times its original budget.

Opposite below: The church's bell-ringers are pictured here in 1956. The group have a fascinating history stretching back to the formation of the St Thomas's Bell-ringing Society in 1879. Early rules required that bell-ringers assembled in the belfry at the appointed hour or a fine of one old penny would be imposed. Any bell-ringer who used profane language faced a hefty fine of sixpence.

Above: An interior view of the church from the 1930s. Beneath its lofty columns the church accommodates 1,020 worshippers, enough seats to have accommodated one in three of the population when the church was consecrated in 1869. Amongst the stained glass windows is a pane dedicated to the Revd Hugh Morgan, the late vicar of Rhyl who had driven forward plans for the construction of the church.

The choir of St John's church, c. 1906. St John's church has now closed and its parishioners worship at St Thomas's church.

The view inside the interior of Our Lady of the Assumption church, c. 1916. The Roman Catholic church was established here in 1863.

Kinmel Street, c. 1909. Although it looks very tranquil in this scene, the road became notorious in 1960 for the gruesome 'mummy in the cupboard' murder case. For over twenty years a Kinmel Street landlady kept the mummified body of a former tenant who had died at her lodging house. She was subsequently acquitted of murder charges but found guilty of having fraudulently continued claiming the deceased lodger's pension.

The Royal Alexandra Hospital, pictured shortly after its official opening in 1902 by Prince George, then Prince of Wales. The hospital was built on the site of an earlier and much smaller children's hospital founded in 1872. The new hospital was one of the largest in Britain and accommodated patients from across the country.

The picture postcard producers of yesteryear seemed to have photographed everything for reproduction as picture postcards. Thankfully they captured this everyday scene inside the hospital's Gertrude Ffoulkes ward, *c.* 1909.

THE CHAPEL OF
THE ROYAL ALEXANDRA
HOSPITAL, RHYL.

Many sick patients sought solace in their faith and the hospital had the ability to accommodate those needs. This is a view of the small chapel inside the Royal Alexandra Hospital, *c.* 1909.

The first bungalow ever built in Rhyl still stands on Tynewydd Road. The historic house dates from about 1865 and was known as The Bungalow, Rhyl – not surprisingly given it was the only structure of its type throughout the district.

The Pen-y-Don Tower is one of the most striking landmarks of Rhyl's seafront and was originally used as a semaphore signalling station for steam packet boats operating between the Foryd Harbour and Liverpool. Sir Edward German is reputed to have composed his famous work *Merrie England* from the tea house that once stood alongside the tower.

The first road crossing of the Clwyd had been built in 1861, operated as a private toll bridge; it had become dilapidated over the decades and was eventually pulled down to make way for this fine structure. This picture postcard view shows the new Foryd Bridge, opened in 1932 to replace the crumbling toll structure.

Another view of the new Foryd Bridge. The £66,000 bridge was built by Dorman Long, who were later to build Runcorn Bridge and Sydney Harbour Bridge.

The growth of mass tourism for the family gave rise to the emergence of holiday camps and Rhyl was well placed to have its own camps. This rare view shows Sunnyvale Holiday Camp in 1936. The camp was located by the Foryd Bridge and still survives today, although now operating as a caravan park.

Another camp that became well established in the 1930s was the Elway Hall Holiday Home and Camp. It was established in the spacious grounds of Elway Hall and is pictured here about 1935.

SOME OF THE BUNGALOWS AT ELWY HALL
HOLIDAY HOME AND CAMP. RHYL.

Anyone for tennis? Various sports and games were provided for holidaymakers at Elway Hall Holiday Camp. This scene shows some of the small holiday chalets in the grounds of the camp in 1935.

MEN'S CONVALESCENT HOME, RHYL.

With its reputation for sunshine and fine sea air Rhyl was an obvious place of rest for convalescents, and several homes were established in the Victorian resort. The Men's Convalescent Institute opened on Bedford Street in 1856. It originally had fifty-six beds for convalescents but was expanded over time to accommodate as many as 140 patients. This photograph of the institute was taken in 1907.

The institute was funded by voluntary subscriptions, donations and a nominal contribution from patients. Figures for 1914 reveal its incredible popularity: 1,024 convalescents were admitted, staying a total of 2,787 weeks. This picture postcard view dates from about 1902.

A gathering of convalescents at the Men's Convalescent Institute, 1928.

The Women's Convalescent Home opened in 1875, established from an enlargement of Morfa Hall, the historic building that had been Rhyl's first visitor accommodation from the 1820s. This fine building afforded good sea views until the Westminster Hotel was built. From 1949 to 1969 the building also housed the historic Ysgol Dewi Sant.

William & John Jones' Convalescent Home, *c.* 1926.

Patients and nursing staff of the William & John Jones' Convalescent Home pose for a photograph in the garden in 1926.

Many trade unions, charitable organisations and kind-hearted employers operated seaside convalescent homes. This is Colet House, which for many years operated as the South Yorkshire Miners' Convalescent Home.

Colet House School, 1906.

Originally created by a local seed merchant called John Jones, the eight-acre Botanic Gardens were later purchased by a syndicate of enthusiasts and opened to the public. This picture of the gardens is from 1922.

three

That's
Entertainment

Above: Minstrel troupes and other performing Pierrots have been appearing along Rhyl's seafront since the 1860s. One of the best known of the earliest groups was E.H. Williams' 'Merrie Men'. Established in 1899, they were the largest Merrie Men show in the kingdom. No other group boasted eighteen professional performers of comedy, song and dance.

Left: Mr E.H. Williams poses for a portrait in 1901. The proprietor of the Merrie Men was a local of Rhyl and a prominent talent of the Rhyl Dramatic Club.

Published by A. & H. Sandoe, Rhyl. 2044

MERRIE MEN.   E. H. Williams Famous Rhyl Merrie Men.

Bonne réussite - bon courage - Marie

This picture postcard from 1904 shows the famous Merrie Men alongside their seafront stage.

As noticeable in this 1904 view, open-air performances were capable of drawing huge crowds. In wet weather performances switched to the Town Hall and it is questionable if this particular crowd of watchers could have all fitted into the building had the heavens opened.

In 1907 Gilbert Rogers and his Jovial Jesters followed the Merrie Men into residency at Rhyl. Gilbert Rogers broke with convention in 1916 when he added a female entertainer to the traditionally all-male shows. He is seen here seated centrally in this 1912 publicity card.

Jovial Jesters, Rhyl

The Jovial Jesters pictured at their sea seafront pitch, *c.* 1910. Three performances a day were staged on the beach. Their captivating routine of dance, song and comedy sketches continued on until the 1920s.

Gilbert Rogers and his Jovial Jesters, 1907. From left to right, back row: Derek Knowles, Norman Walker, Jack Jewell, George Gilder, Dan Brooks. Front row: Reggie Heaton, Gilbert Rogers, Wilfred Knowles.

A rare view of the Jovial Jesters amidst a song and dance routine, 1909. Deck chairs for the performances were hired at one penny.

This promenade view shows the Grand Pavilion. Opened in 1891, this magnificent venue boasted the world's largest wind organ. The twenty-eight-ton instrument had 3,095 pipes – stretching to five miles if they were to have been put end to end. Arthur Cheetham screened some of the earliest moving image films here before the Grand Pavilion was destroyed by fire in 1901.

THE PIER, RHYL.

The Amphitheatre, c. 1938. The theatre adjoined the entrance to Rhyl Pier and will forever be synonymous with the name of Billy Manders and his performing company the 'Quaintesques'. The entertainer took a lease on the theatre in 1921 and his variety performers staged summer seasons there for the coming forty-two years.

Built in 1921 the Coliseum continued Rhyl's romance with open-air theatre. This view of the Coliseum is from 1926. The Pier Pavilion offers a superb backdrop to the 660-seat venue.

The Coliseum was best known for the residency of Billy Churchill and his 'Jolly Boys'. Churchill was a well-respected entertainer who also managed concerts at Llandudno's Happy Valley. The white-capped Jolly Boys can be seen mixing in with the audience in this 1924 picture.

Above: Another timeless portrait of the deck-chaired holidaymakers at the Coliseum, 1924.

Below: Will Parkin took over the management of the Jolly Boys in 1927. One of his summertime shows is pictured here on the Coliseum stage. The 'Optimists' show was performed three times a day and ran for many years.

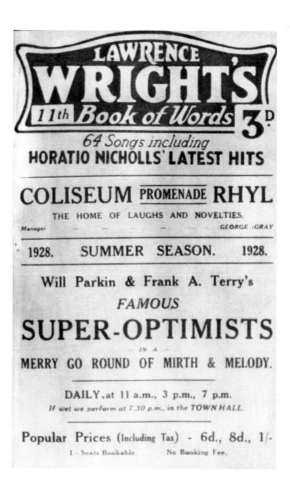

Right: A poster advertising the 1928 summer season at the Coliseum.

Below: A rare view of the Amphitheatre in the 1950s. Advertising boards for the Quaintesques variety shows adorn the front of the building. The 700-seat venue eventually became known as the Gaiety Theatre. It closed in 1991.

Above: The Quaintesques in 1941.
Back row: Harry Mitchell-Craig,
Micky Trenton, Paolo Zaharoff,
Billie Manders, Jimmy Oliver, Derek
Down, Edward Davies. Front row:
Mollie Winston, Muriel Murray, Held
Cardiac, Doris Nil, Barbara Ford,
Barbara Caginess, Barbara Adams.

Left: Billy Manders pictured in
one of his many stage costumes.
He was particularly famous for
his performances as a female
impersonator.

Above: The passion and splendour of the Quaintesques show must have been quite something as they continued in residence for many decades. They carried on working as a company following Billy Manders' death in 1950, and continued staging shows at the Amphitheatre until 1962. This picture shows the Quaintesques during a stage performance in the 1950s.

Right: The cover of the theatre programme for Dick Whittington, Billie Manders' Grand Christmas Pantomime at the Pavilion in 1936.

The PAVILION THEATRE, RHYL

Entertainments Manager   C. PRIESTLEY EDWARDS

For One Week Only. Commencing MONDAY, DEC. 28th. 1936.
Nightly at 7.30 p.m.   Matinees Daily (except Monday) at 2.30.

BILLIE MANDERS
Presents His Grand Christmas Pantomime
"Dick Whittington"

THE SUN-TRAP OF NORTH WALES
Sunny RHYL

Above: The Pavilion, *c.* 1945. The domed building arguably remains the most iconic landmark in Rhyl's history. Following its opening in 1908 it was the principal theatre of the town and attracted all the big star names of the day. The Pavilion was demolished in 1974.

Left: Many celebrities have trodden the boards of Rhyl's famous Pavilion including Arthur Askey, the diminutive comic actor who was a treasure chest of catchphrases.

Tommy Trinder was one of Britain's foremost entertainers during the Second World War and another star to have had a summer season at the Pavilion. In the 1950s Trinder was probably the biggest celebrity on television, even comparing the hugely popular show Sunday Night at the London Palladium.

Left: Paul Robeson gave a one-off performance at the Pavilion in 1934 to coincide with local promotions for the annual Co-operative Congress. Robeson was a singer and actor of world-renown who later in his career turned his attentions to the American civil rights movement.

Below: Prince's International Circus, 1956. Their circus big top was in residence at the Pavilion for thirteen summer seasons until 1961.

Above: Opened in 1902, the Queen's Palace was the supreme expression of Rhyl's grandeur as a resort. The ornate four-storey pleasure palace was billed as the Theatre of Varieties and included a first class theatre, ballroom, shopping arcade, zoo, restaurant and hotel. There was a tropical roof garden under its dome and an underground Venetian canal in the basement, complete with gondolas for best effect! This view shows an exterior view of the Queen's Palace in 1906.

Below: The interior of the Grand Ballroom. The 6,000ft of parquet flooring was capable of accommodating 2,000 dancing couples.

ROOF GARDEN, QUEEN'S PALACE, RHYL

Above: The tropics come to Rhyl. A view of the tropical Ashanti jungle village in the Queen's Palace. From a small viewing tower above the Palace's huge glass dome visitors could see the Irish coastline, the Isle of Man and the peaks of Snowdonia.

Left: Do you recognise this former stage actress from the heyday of the Queen's Palace Theatre? This is a young Betty Driver pictured in the 1940s. She went on to find fame as Betty Turpin, the evergreen barmaid of the Rovers Return in *Coronation Street.*

Opposite below: Another fine mess. The theatre and ballroom were completely destroyed by fire in November 1907, bringing to a close one of the most beautiful entertainment venues of North Wales. The cost of damage was estimated at £70,000, no small sum in those days, and only a minor part of it could be recovered by insurance.

Above: The iconic figures of Laurel and Hardy once graced the theatre stage of the Queen's Palace. The famous comic duo made a memorable visit to the Queen's Palace in July 1952.

Amateur dramatics have played an important tradition in Rhyl's entertainment history. This scene shows the stage set of the farcical comedy *Jane*, performed by the Rhyl Amateur Dramatic Society in 1911. The play performed to packed houses at the New Pavilion.

The Rhyl Silver Band has been part of the musical heart of the town for many decades and they continue to perform at important local civic occasions. This band picture is from 1929.

A picture of the Rhyl Silver Band performing in the late 1950s.

ℝitz BALLROOM PROMENADE RHYL Tel. 2457

DANCING

Friday 19th July	**'THE BEATLES'**	Saturday 20th July
8.30—12.30	ADMISSION 17/6 Late Transport	8—11.45

MONDAY TO FRIDAY: 2.30—4.30.   **ADMISSION 2/-.**

TWIST 'N' MADISON AFTERNOONS

MONDAYS   WEDNESDAYS

TWIST 'N' MADISON NIGHTS

8—11 p.m.	ADMISSION 3/-	8.30—11.30 p.m.

An advert for the Beatles show at the Ritz Ballroom. The 'fab four' played two sell-out nights at the popular promenade ballroom in 1963, just prior to recording sessions for their second album. The Ritz was a popular nightclub venue until being destroyed by fire in 1968.

The Odeon Cinema is clearly seen to the right in this scene from the 1950s. The Odeon opened in 1937 and was capable of seating 1,500 cinema-goers. In 1953 the picture house had been the only public venue to offer a full-length viewing of the Queen's Coronation at Westminster Abbey.

A modern view of the Art Deco Odeon building, now housing Apollo Bingo.

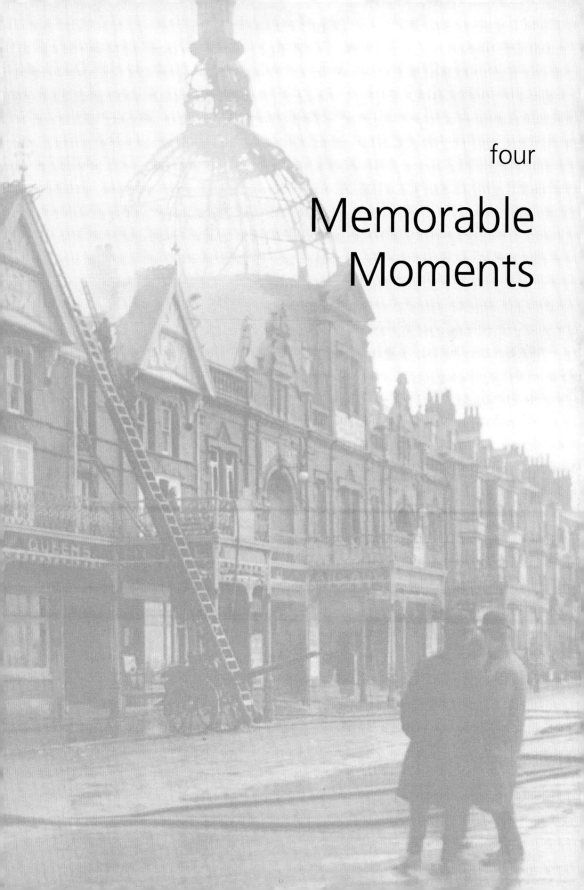

four

Memorable
Moments

Rhyl had the good fortune of accommodating some of the finest theatres of North Wales but sadly equal misfortune in seeing each destroyed. This promenade view from November 1907 captures the aftermath of the tragic fire that destroyed the Queen's Palace. The night before a huge crowd of onlookers had gathered in disbelief at the loss of the mighty entertainment palace.

This sketch from 1930 shows work progressing on the construction of the Foryd Bridge. This was the first toll-free public road crossing of the Clwyd and, almost eighty years later, still forms the main route into Rhyl from Kinmel Bay.

This rare view from August 1885 shows the laying of the foundation stone for St John's church in Wellington Road. Top hats and pleated dresses were visibly the fashion of the day.

In 1903 the Wild West Show of world famous frontiersman Buffalo Bill came to town for a one night performance that commenced his Welsh tour. William F. Cody, as Buffalo Bill was actually named, stirred considerable excitement in Rhyl. He was an authentic pony express rider, American Civil War soldier, buffalo hunter and Indian fighter and his swashbuckling Wild West Show easily caught the public's imagination. Buffalo Bill always looked resplendent in his fringed buckskins and silver spurs and he remains one of the most distinguished performers ever to appear at Rhyl.

Right: This rare cigarette card image pictures the celebrated stunt swimmer Tommy Burns. He developed notoriety for performing dangerous stunts even before his arrival in 1897 for a season of exhibition diving at Rhyl. Burns died in a freak accident whilst plunging off Rhyl's Victoria Pier. The watching crowd had failed to realise the swimmer's difficulties and applauded wildly his last fateful stunt.

Below: Royal occasions have been celebrated with exuberant enthusiasm in Rhyl and this was especially true of the Coronation of King George V in 1911. Streets were gaily decorated in bunting and streamers and this huge public procession made its way from the Town Hall to the Pier Pavilion. More than half the population of the town either participated in or watched the procession, seen here on the promenade. Partying continued on into the evening with a firework display over the promenade's pier.

Inspection of the South Wales Brigade
By
Major General E. Dixon. Rhyl

Connie Banning
May Queen RHYL 1913

Above: This dramatic view from 1915 shows an inspection of the South Wales Brigade by Maj.-Gen. E. Dixon. Rhyl was an important billeting location for troops during the First World War and a great deal of pride was taken in the support that local residents offered to the troops. At the time when this picture was taken more than 5,000 troops were billeted in guest houses and family homes.

Left: Another excuse for pomp and pageantry was the crowing of the May queen. Rhyl's annual May Day began in 1891, when Christchurch schoolgirl Beta Barger became the first May queen. During the day a parade of gaily decorated horse drawn carriages would carry the May queen through the streets and large crowds assembled to join in with the festivities. Pictured here is Connie Banning, the 1913 May queen.

Opposite: Mary Stanley Roose poses in this studio portrait after having been crowned Rhyl's forty-second May queen, 1933.

Above: The assembled court of Elva Ballyn Davies, Rhyl's 1938 May queen. Elva's special day involved a procession though the town with decorated floats, ceremonial bands and Morris dancers. She was crowned later at a coronation ceremony in the Pier Pavilion.

Below: The flower-drenched float of May queen Elva Ballyn Davies, pictured in 1938 outside the Pier Hotel.

Right: Sheila Acton, Rhyl's 1945 May queen, pictured alongside her lady-in-waiting, Audrey Ballyn Davies.

Below: Rita Landi's Choir, pictured in 1936 with the trophy they won at the Chester Music Festival. The choir was well known for its superb vocal harmonies and won many competitions.

School outings have always been an important aspect of the school year and they never needed to be to far-flung destinations to inspire the enthusiasm of pupils. This happy group of children from Christchurch school is pictured on an outing to Brookes Farm on Rhuddlan Road in 1939.

Victory in Europe heralded ecstatic celebrations in Rhyl. Thousands of people took to the streets, church bells rang and parades were held in the town. This 1945 view shows the victory parade passing by the Regal Cinema on the High Street.

Many streets held victory parties to mark the passing of the Second World War. This particular gathering was taken at Westfield Road in August 1945.

Do you recognise a bonny baby? This gathering of local children shows contestants in Rhyl Carnival's beauty competition. The picture was taken in the late 1950s.

Left: After the Second World War beauty competitions quickly emerged as a favourite form of seaside entertainment. Morecambe was the first resort to hold a competition but Rhyl was not far behind with its own search for Miss Rhyl. Pictured here is Cllr Rose, chairman of Rhyl Urban Council, congratulating Miss Rhyl, Audrey Davies, on her subsequent crowning as Miss Flintshire. To the left is Irene MacDonald, Miss Rhyl 1948.

Below: Youngsters from Thorpe Street, Brighton Road and Bath Street assemble outside the Brunswick Schoolroom for this 1953 street party. Joyous scenes celebrated the Queen's Coronation in streets and public buildings across the town. At home, crowds gathered around television sets to view the amazing scenes from Westminster Abbey. The first babies born in Rhyl on Coronation Day were aptly named Elizabeth and Philip, twin children of Mr and Mrs Jack Muff of Vale Road.

Right: No sooner had the coronation celebrations subsided and the Queen herself put in a personal appearance at Rhyl. In July 1953 she came to attend the Eisteddfod festivities and drove though the town in the company of Prince Philip. A crowd greater than the entire population of Flintshire lined the new monarch's route. This rare picture shows the royal car passing by Jonson's in the aptly named Queen Street.

Below: Carnival Day in 1969 and the 'Dunlop Man' can be seen passing along High Street.

Left: Another Carnival Day procession: this time the voluntary uniformed services can be seen parading along Wellington Road, *c.* 1947.

Bolow: Not all displays of Rhyl's social pomp and pageantry are in public. This scene shows the local Grand Order of Buffaloes in 1973.

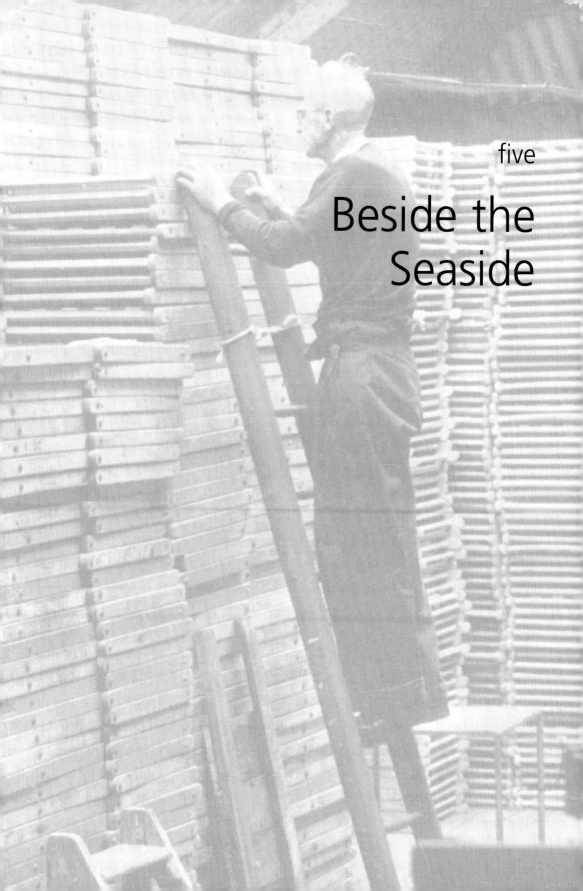

five

Beside the
Seaside

With its fine seafront and an array of accommodation it was easy to see why the Victorian resort attracted visitors in such large numbers. For many people, the beach was the perfect place to enjoy the sunshine. However, it is interesting to note how everyone is fully clothed in this picture from 1910.

Another view of the busy sands, c. 1913.

Spades at the ready. Holidaymakers pose for a photograph before embarking on some fun on the sands, *c.* 1922.

Trousers are rolled up to the knees in this period postcard image from about 1911. In the background is Rhyl Pier.

Children play alongside the water's edge in this beach scene, *c.* 1920.

Rhyl's historic Victoria Pier opened in 1867 and for almost a century was a key feature of the town's seafront. The 2,355ft long pier offered various attractions including diving competitions, pier shops and kiosks, slot machines, and the Bijou Pavilion Theatre. This view of the pier was taken in the late 1950s, just a few years before it was declared unsafe and closed to public use.

It is interesting to note the beach fashions on show in this image from the early 1900s, long pleated dresses and straw hats are clearly the flavour of the day. The large building seen on the pier is the Bijou Pavilion Theatre. In common with the curse affecting some other entertainment venues in old Rhyl, the Bijou was later destroyed by fire.

Another view of the pier taken from the beach. In its early years Victoria Pier was a staging point for passenger steamers to Llandudno and Liverpool's Pier Head. When this picture was taken in 1911 a return fare to Liverpool cost three shillings.

This extremely rare image from the 1880s shows the promenade pictured from the pier.

Along with holidaymakers who came back year after year, local personalities gave the seaside a strong sense of community. For many years deckchair attendant Herbert Davies was a well-known figure on the seafront, easily spotted wearing his cap and cloak. He is pictured here in 1961.

At the end of another hard day of hiring deckchairs on the beach, Herbert Davies returns all the chairs to Rhyl Urban District Council's deckchair store, 1961.

Deckchairs were not always the favoured means of resting on Rhyl beach. Prior to the 1950s, basket chairs were popularly used on the sands. These large cumbersome seats can be seen in this picture postcard from 1928.

Some couples and families would put two basket chairs together to create a more private, shaded spot for themselves on the beach. Basket chairs are much in evidence in this picture from the 1920s. The building to the right is Forrest's Ice Cream stall.

3778. PROMENADE & SANDS.W. RHYL

Other curiosities viewed in this picture from 1910 are the bathing huts on the beach. Owned and operated by the Vaughan family, these contraptions were hired to help spare the blushes of bathers. Inside the wheeled huts customers changed into beach attire before horses pulled the hut to the water's edge.

A line of bathing huts is seen along the West Shore, *c.* 1926.

Mixed Bathing at Rhyl

This early picture postcard intends to offer a comical portrayal of mixed bathing at Rhyl but it touches upon a serious issue. From 1865 by-laws prevented both sexes from mixing together on the beach and a roped line offered demarcation. The by-laws were so draconian it was a wonder anyone could bathe at all. Rules were only relaxed before 7 a.m. when bathers were unlikely to want to take to the sea.

More bathing huts and basket chairs are seen in this picture from about 1910. The wooden building beyond the bathing huts is the lifeboat station, built here on the beach in 1897.

Trips aboard pleasure boats were once popular with visitors. This picture postcard view from 1924 suggests wet feet might have been all part and parcel of the experience.

Nobody knows who first introduced donkeys onto the beach but generations of children were thankful they did. This group of holidaymakers is pictured on the sands, *c.* 1910.

Another group photograph of donkey riders, showing the pier in the background, c. 1912.

This Edwardian view of donkeys on Rhyl beach is fascinating for what we can see in the background. The small octagonal building was the Camera Obscura. It worked by reflecting mirrored images from a rooftop lens down onto a circular turntable within the darkened room. Many seaside towns had Camera Obscuras, allowing visitors to see moving coloured pictures of the scene outside in an era when the moving image was only beginning to be developed.

It is not just donkeys that have found a home on the beach. This rare picture from 1929 shows two thoroughbred racehorses in training on the sands. To the left is 'Star of Argos' and on the right is 'Mizzen Mast.'

There is not much likelihood of horse riding in these conditions. This picture from around 1900 shows high tide on the shore.

six

All at Sea

The Foryd is the historic maritime harbour around which much of Rhyl's early history centred. It was once a royal harbour, well placed to become the gateway to the Clwyd Valley. The harbour was a popular goods port and all sorts of commodities were imported and exported from its quays, not least of all Rhyl's earliest tourists. The landing stages here were being used by Liverpool paddle steamers from as early as 1830 and daily services disembarked visitors from Liverpool's Pier Head. This picture postcard view of the Foryd dates from about 1910.

The harbour was a popular goods port and small merchant quays were built along both banks. Until 1959 the area was also serviced by a railway line, often known as the Quarry Line. It was used predominantly for exporting limestone from St George Quarry. The railway is not noticeable in this 1928 picture postcard but what is clearly visible beyond the schooner is the timber yard of the well-known merchant Charles Jones.

This stunning waterside scene shows a three-masted schooner in tow at the Foryd, *c.* 1912.

Spectators have always been drawn to the harbour, especially so for the launching of boats or to greet the arrival of steamships. By the time this photograph was taken in 1914 people were also enjoying the spectacle of sailing craft.

When this picture was taken in the early 1950s sailing ships were only an occasional sight at the Foryd. The harbour had slowly silted up and small craft made it difficult for cargo ships to manoeuvre.

A view from the harbour looking towards Rhyl. The famous Pier Pavilion can be seen in the distance.

High and dry. Sailing craft moored on the mudflats in 1951.

A modern view of the Foryd in 2006. There are now as many pleasure boats as ever before.

The second Foryd Bridge pictured here in the late 1950s. The bridge is one of the iconic symbols of the area, adjoining Rhyl with Kinmel Bay.

A breezy seafront scene, *c.* 1952.

HOVERCRAFT.

RHYL TO WALLASEY. CARRYING CAPACITY 24 PASSENGERS. CRUISING SPEED 60 MPH.

International headlines were made in July 1962 with trials at Rhyl of the world's first commercial hovercraft. During that summer the Vickers VA3 Hovercraft operated scheduled services between Rhyl and Wallasey. The experimental vessel was capable of cruising at 60mph, taking just thirty-two minutes to cross Liverpool Bay.

This rare photograph shows the arrival of the Vickers Hovercraft in 1962. Regrettably the historic service was blighted by mechanical difficulties and the vessel failed to maintain a consistent service. In one near-disastrous incident it even drifted from its Rhyl moorings and had to be rescued by the lifeboat to prevent it being wrecked at Rhyl seafront. The hovercraft was moved to Southampton in 1966 and unceremoniously blown up in an explosive experiment. This unique aspect of Rhyl's history now lies on the bed of the Solent.

The Shipwrecked Mariners' Society founded Rhyl's lifeboat service in 1852. The first lifeboat was a relatively unstable eight-oar rowing boat named *Gwylan-y-Mor*. Tragically she capsized with the loss of all six crew on what had been her second active rescue. One of the best known lifeboats to have subsequently seen service at Rhyl was the *Caroline Richardson* pictured here in 1913 being pulled ashore by horses. She saw service between 1897 and 1939, the longest period of active service of any of the lifeboats stationed at Rhyl over the past 150 years.

The launching in 1965 of the lifeboat *Anthony Robert Marshall*. By this time the services of horses were dispersed with in favour of powerful tractors, capable of launching lifeboats straight into the raging sea.

Lifeboats have always drawn a crowd of spectators to the seafront and the lifeboat station. This 1965 picture shows the scene outside the station as the Former tractor is used to bring the lifeboat out onto exercise.

The lifeboat *Anthony Robert Marshall* was the most prolific lifesaver of all the lifeboats to serve at Rhyl. It was in service from 1949 to 1968 and during that time launched 102 times, saving no fewer than fifty-one lives. It was the *Anthony Robert Marshall* that had gone to the aid of the stricken Vickers Hovercraft in 1962, gaining the distinction of being the first ever lifeboat to aid a distressed hovercraft.

A view of *Resurgam*, the world's oldest powered submarine. Invented by George Garrett, the pioneering submersible sank off Rhyl in 1880. It has been moored at the Foryd Harbour the evening before its fateful journey and remained unseen until 1995, when divers discovered it five miles off the Rhyl coast.

Boats have not only sailed to and from the town, Rhyl even sailed the seas. This is *HMS Rhyl*, the Rothesay-class Frigate that saw service for the Royal Navy from 1960. The 2,380-ton ship had an active service life, serving on the Beira Patrol that helped impose sanctions against Ian Smith's Rhodesia. During the 1970s *HMS Rhyl* had acted as a fishery protection vessel in the so-called 'Cod Wars'.

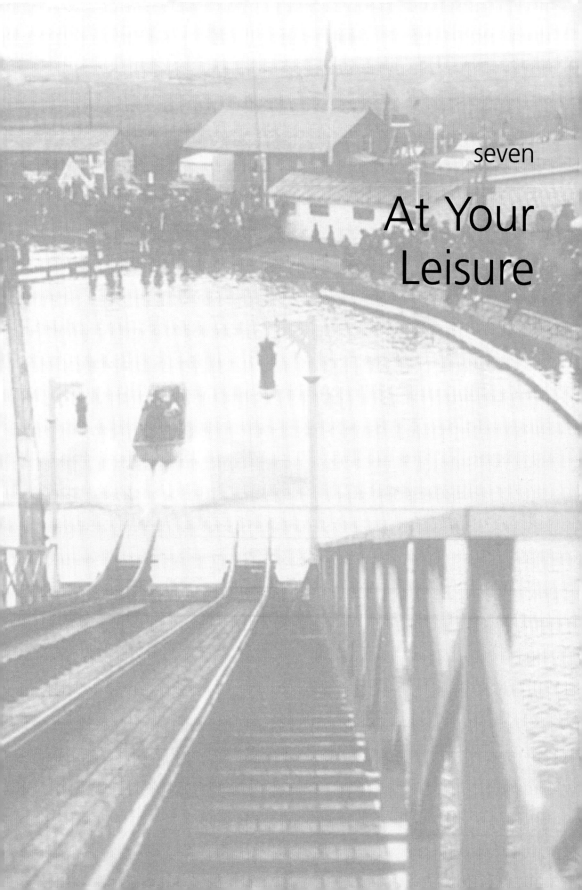

seven

At Your Leisure

Recreation and sport form an important part of any town's past and that is equally true of a resort town like Rhyl. One of the first facilities established by the new Rhyl Urban District Council was the creation of the Marine Lake. Built at a cost of £10,500 the scheme was fraught with criticism and financial setbacks before opening in 1895. This picture postcard view shows the landing stages, *c.* 1909.

The Marine Lake extended over forty acres and had 1,300ft of embankment. In this scene a lone rowing boat takes to the placid waters, *c.* 1911.

The landing stages of the lake, with the Marine Lake Amusement Park seen in the background, *c.* 1913. It was one of the oldest and most successful fairgrounds in North Wales until its closure in the 1960s.

A view of the amusement park seen from the water chute. The roller coaster to the right was built in 1920 by the celebrated roller coaster designer Albert Barnes, and it was one of the highest funfair rides in Britain, becoming something of a landmark for many miles around. In the background, note the open seafront near to the Foryd. This area was later developed with the Ocean Beach Fairground.

The water chute was perhaps the best-known attraction of Rhyl's Edwardian fairground. Built in 1908 this attraction drew crowds of spectators. It operated with flat-bottomed boats being hauled up to the top of the chute, before being released to career down into the lake. The water chute eventually closed as a result of a fatal accident.

This rare view looking down the water chute provides a good impression of the surrounding area in 1911. Other attractions included the tunnel of love, known as the 'Waterways of Mars', and the Marine Lake Miniature Railway.

The Marine Lake Miniature Railway was the showpiece of the area. Originally billed as 'the little trains' it opened in 1911 and was an instant success, attracting queues at peak season. The first miniature steam engine to use the fifteen-inch gauge track was the *Prince Edward of Wales*, named in honour of the new prince's impending investiture. Another engine brought into service in 1913 was *George V*, pictured here on the circular lakeside track.

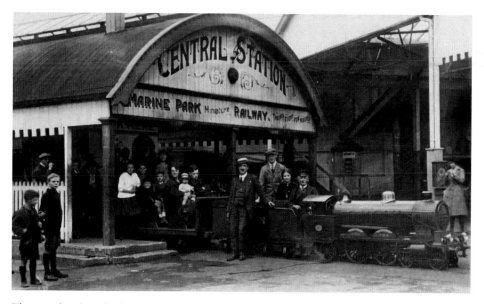

The sound and smell of whistlers and steam had gripped schoolchildren as they entered the Marine Lake Amusement Park. Central Station was the boarding place for passengers and from here the track ran through a tunnel under the roller coaster before encircling almost one mile of the lake.

Full steam ahead. This picture postcard view from 1958 shows a train fully laden with passengers. At its peak in the 1920s the miniature railway was used by thousands of passengers a day.

This posed photograph shows Inspector Charles Waterfield alongside the steam engine *Prince Edward of Wales*. Waterfield made a name for himself during the First World War. Such was his devotion to his country that the sixty-six year-old man enlisted in the army, wrongly telling enlisting officers that he was forty-three years of age. Inspector Waterfield survived the war but the steam engine's days were numbered: she was sold to Margate Miniature Railway in 1920.

Another steam engine races around the lakeside in 1930. The Miniature Railway finally closed in 1969 but some years later interest in it was revived and a new track relaid. Since 2001 the future of Rhyl's historic miniature railway has been entrusted to the Rhyl Steam Preservation Trust and its enthusiastic volunteers help keep the little trains in operation.

Rhyl District Football Club's team photograph in the 1912-13 season. Rhyl's amateur teams played under a variety of names in the late nineteenth century, before Rhyl United moved to Belle Vue in 1900 to form the origins of what would become the 'Lilywhites' – Rhyl Football Club.

Rhyl Football Club was officially founded in 1883 and after almost 125 years it is still one of the best-known names in non-league football. The club became a power in Welsh football in the 1920s, reaching the Welsh Cup Finals in 1927 and 1930. This particular team photograph dates from about this time, before Rhyl began their first spell of playing in the English football leagues.

Hockey has enjoyed considerable acclaim in Rhyl's sporting past. Rhyl Hockey Club was founded in 1888 and is one of the oldest clubs in the UK. It famously organised the world's first international hockey match. The fixture between Wales and Ireland was played at the Winter Gardens in 1895. This photograph shows the club's team in 1938.

The Grosvenor Ladies Hockey Club, pictured in the early 1950s.

Crown Green Bowls was a popular game on the East Parade. During the summer season bowlers competed for various trophies, ending each September with the Slater Tournament.

Rhyl's showpiece open-air swimming pool opened in 1930, and astonishingly 223,000 people passed through its turnstiles in the opening season. It has the distinction of being the first major outdoor pool to stage competition swimming. Its popularity with swimmers was so great that special day excursions had to be operated to cater for the influx of visitors. This view from 1943 suggests that not even the war could dampen the spirit of Rhyl's sunshine bathers.

The huge seawater pool had seating for 2,500 spectators and 380 cubicles for swimmers. Various events were held at the pool including beauty competitions. The pool is pictured here in the 1950s.

eight

Transported
Back in Time

The railway age came to Rhyl in 1848, spurring the expansion of the town. The fledgling resort was given another boost when the Vale of Clwyd Railway opened in 1858. Such was the influx of summer visitors that the station had to be enlarged in 1878. The intention of the town's commissioners was for Rhyl to have 'a station as equally beautiful as that of Llandudno Junction.' This picture postcard shows the enlarged railway station as it appeared in 1908.

Rhyl became one of the busiest railway stations on the Chester to Holyhead line. In the summer season large numbers of passengers disembarked at Rhyl, feeding an almost incessant thirst for boarding houses and hotels. However, by the time this photograph was taken in 1968 Rhyl's platforms were falling silent. People were now taking to their family cars, helping to make crowded platforms a thing of the past.

Spend a Day at the Seaside

SPECIAL EXCURSIONS

TO

SUNNY RHYL

Monday, 26th July, 1954
Wednesday, 28th July, 1954

FROM	TIMES OF DEPARTURE		RETURN FARE THIRD CLASS
	26th JULY	28th JULY	
	a m	a m	s d
WREXHAM CEN.	11 10	11 05	5/0
„ EX.	—	11 09	5/0
GWERSYLET	11 16	11 14	5/0
CEFNYBEDD	11 20	11 19	5/0
CAERGWRLE C.	11 23	11 23	5/0
HOPE VILLAGE	11 27	11 27	5/0
PENYFFORDD	11 33	11 33	4/9
PADESWOOD & B.	11 41	11 39	4/6
LLONG	11 44	11 42	4/8†
MOLD	11 50	11 47	4/5†
	p m	p m	
RHYL arr.	12 55	12 55	—

† Summertime Cheap Day Tickets.

RETURN ARRANGEMENTS

Passengers return same day by special train leaving Rhyl at 8.10 p.m. on Monday, 26th July, and at 8.15 p.m. on Wednesday, 28th July.

Children under three years of age, free ; three years and under fourteen, half fares.

These tickets are issued subject to the British Transport Commission's published Regulations and Conditions applicable to British Railways exhibited at their Stations or obtainable free of charge at station booking offices.

Further information will be supplied on application to the Stations, Agencies, or to F. H. FISHER, District Traffic Superintendent, Chester. Tel. Chester 24680 (Ext. 28).

July, 1954   K 533

BRITISH RAILWAYS

B. Haram & Co. Ltd., Printers,
61 Hamilton Street, Birkenhead.

A British Railways' flyer advertising rail excursions to 'Sunny Rhyl' in 1954.

SEASIDE EXCURSIONS

WEDNESDAYS
3rd and 17th JUNE
TO
RHYL

FROM	DEPARTURE TIMES		RETURN FARES Second Class	DUE BACK	
	3rd	17th		3rd	17th
	a.m.	a.m.	s. d.	p.m.	p.m.
BIRMINGHAM New Street	10 35	10 35	15/-	10 5	10 5
SMETHWICK Rolfe Street	10 45	10 45		9 50	9 50
SPON LANE	10 50	10 50	14/6	9 45	9 46
OLDBURY & BROMFORD LANE	10 54	10 53		9 40	9 42
ALBION	10 57	..		9 35	
DUDLEY	10*45	10*50		9*40	9*45
DUDLEY PORT	11 0	11 0	14/-	9 30	9 35
TIPTON Owen Street	..	11 5		..	9 30
COSELEY Deepfields	..	11 9			9 26
WALSALL	10†45	10†45		9†35	9†57
WOLVERHAMPTON High Level	11 15	11 15	13/6	9 15	9 15
STAFFORD	11 45	11 44	10/6	8 50	8 50
	p.m.	p.m.			
RHYL arr.	1 40	1 40	*—Change at Dudley Port		
	p.m.	p.m.			
Return same day at	6 45	7 10	†—Change at Wolverhampton High Level		

NOTICE AS TO CONDITIONS

These tickets are issued subject to the British Transport Commission's published Regulations and Conditions applicable to British Railways exhibited at their stations or obtainable free of charge at station booking offices.

CHILDREN under three years of age, free; three years and under fourteen, half-fares.

TICKETS CAN BE OBTAINED IN ADVANCE AT THE STATIONS AND AGENCIES

Further information will be supplied on application to Stations, official Railway Agents, or to D. S. Hart, District Passenger Manager, New Street Station, Birmingham 2. Telephone: MIDland 2740.

May, 1959   B.R. 35000

LONDON MIDLAND

Staffords, Netherfield

Above: The great steam age is revived in this old snapshot. The LMS steam engine 1108 is seen pulling into Rhyl railway station in July 1941.

Right: A selection of bell-punched tickets for train services at Rhyl. From top to bottom: Rhyl platform ticket, second class single from Llandudno to Rhyl, London & North Western bicycle ticket, third class Liverpool Lime Street to Rhyl via Runcorn.

Opposite: Rhyl was a popular holiday destination with holidaymakers from the Midlands. This bill from 1959 details some of the special seaside excursions operated by London Midland.

The steam locomotive *Elkhound* pictured on the train turntable at Rhyl, *c.* 1938.

This picture postcard view from 1908 shows the Irish mail train racing through Rhyl. In the background you can just about see the Claremont Hydro.

A reminder of the early days of private transport in Rhyl. To the right in this 1902 picture is the Connah Hiring Depot. Motor cars and cycles could be hired from here, allowing visitors their own personal means of exploring the district. Note the horse and carriages to the left, waiting outside the Queens Hotel.

Charabanc outings were once all part and parcel of a family holiday at Rhyl and Brookes Bros were on hand to operate these services. The three brothers had begun their business about 1900, initially offering horse-drawn excursions around North Wales. They introduced charabanc coach excursions in 1911 and their services became a common sight on Rhyl's roads.

Over the years Brookes Bros extended their fleet of charabanc coaches and began trading under the name of White Rose Motors. This particular group of White Rose excursionists are pictured by Water Street in 1933.

Journeying in open-topped coaches, with solid rubber tyres and a lack of suspension, could hardly have been a comfortable experience. What's more, these White Rose charabancs were capable of a maximum speed of just 12mph! This particular picture was taken outside the Belvoir Hotel in 1928.

The Brookes Brothers continued to extend their interests throughout the 1920s and 1930s and expanded the business to operate coaches, taxis, car hire and furniture removal vans. One of their largest acquisitions was the purchase in 1926 of the rival Rhyl & Potteries Motors. This last charabanc picture shows excursionists outside their company offices in 1925.